I0756235

FINISHING LINE PRESS
www.finishinglinepress.com

IN A PLACE, AT A TIME

poems by

Cheryl Howard

Finishing Line Press
Georgetown, Kentucky

IN A PLACE, AT A TIME

To the people and places of New Mexico I have loved
and those that have loved me back.

ISBN 979-8-89990-509-4 First Edition

ACKNOWLEDGMENTS

An earlier version of "Geography Begins" was published in *Rutas*, a student publication of the University of Texas at El Paso
"Gracias Siempre;" "Driving the Mimbres on a Winter Day;" "Driving With the Spirits/Manejando con los Espiritus" and an earlier version of "Some Memories" appeared in Fixed and Free
"Adobe Words" won an honorable mention award in an annual writing contest sponsored by Desert Exposure

Publisher: Leah Huete de Maines
Editor: Christen Kincaid
Cover Art: Cheryl Howard
Author Photo: Mary Troutman Gates
Cover Design: Elizabeth Maines McCleavy

Order online: www.finishinglinepress.com
also available on amazon.com

Author inquiries and mail orders:
Finishing Line Press
PO Box 1626
Georgetown, Kentucky 40324
USA

Contents

GEOGRAPHY BEGINS

geography begins at home.
with the skin, the bones.
traveling back in time to the ancestors.
forward to what you will.
make of this.

geography becomes clearer with age.
lines demarcating choices, here and there.
separating. milk from cream.
churning, chilled, geography becomes solid.
usable to the mind.
cartographic. this is that.
these are those or us or them.

geography can break down
boundaries melt in every season .
our bodies find their ways
into each other.
we pass time in this fashion.
grow

fluid, as if our wrinkled skins become rivers
flowing over rocks
our bones, into new dimensions

down, always, toward salt for our wounds
toward oceans
taking us tumbled.
to enter the dominion of Phoenician sailors
who navigate by the stars

WHERE THE LLANO MEETS THE SKY

where the llano meets blue sky
where white clouds dive toward horizons
where winds blow unchecked across emptiness
tumbleweeds cross a road to sit in barb-wire fences
where dust becomes a devil, swirls across the land
where storm clouds gather low, purple,
thick with the smell of moisture
and pound cold into your bones
rare rain presses hard into your face
where, in a good year, there's enough
for a few cows or sheep to graze
but not a sure garden or crop
where the sun reigns most days

this is where my ancestors came
from greener places, to throw their lot
into this unforgiving land
from Cherokee to Apache homelands
acres offered by the government
even if it did not belong to them
free.... if only they proved it

what did they love or learn to love?
something strong
because
they never returned to green pastures
I follow in these footsteps
travel these same roads
from red clay to white sand
follow small rivers:
Hondo, Peñasco, Tularosa, Mimbres
from mountains to deserts and back again

I do not own this land, this sky;
it owns me

IN A PLACE

I found you in a place
where language failed
there are many places
like that

most of them hardly noticeable
maybe music
rushes in to fill the emptiness

or the bleeding colors of sunset

the electricity of love and sweat
on skin
under the tongue

the scent taste
of apples or roses
vanilla or Shalimar
green chile roasting in August
Mexican bird of paradise blooms
that fly into alleys of memory

I might have expected
any of these senses
but when I tip-toed in
to this wordless world

there was only you
but from there
we could go anywhere

GRACIAS SIEMPRE

from the south
across the Isleta Bridge
across the Rio Grande
into Albuquerque
a city I have not lived in for more than 30 years
I feel the warm arms of this city
surround me
and suddenly
I am 17 with a footlocker
moving into Hokona Hall
for my freshman year
those years compressing, expanding
into the many years after
the people who became the flannel shirts I wear closely even now
those whose faces became tin types of nostalgia
the books that changed the course of my river's history
places that became sacred by ritual and repetition
myriad futures made possible for a naïve youth

this
this is the city
that hugged me
that held me close while opening my eyes
the city that protected me until I knew
what kind of woman I wanted to become

EAST OAKLAND, 1970-71

East Oakland, you gave me the underbelly
the hood with its pants pulled down
condoms and needles on the Sunday sidewalk
felonious children I taught to swim and came to love
Hell's Angels who idled their engines
when one of them saw it was scaring the dog
Sly and the Family Stone loud
late into the night
Angela Davis poster in the closet

East Oakland, you gave me the crazy of Vietnam
the Oakland Induction Center, where anguished young men
with testicles wrapped in tin foil, garter snakes in their underwear
or emaciated from weeks of starvation
young men desperate to avoid the draft
and the warriors tasked with ignoring this insanity
downed cheap PX beer, smoked Marlboros
told hilarious stories on the weekend
trying to obliterate their own 365 days in country

East Oakland, you gave me the Berkeley brain
and a back way to get there
without ditching the MG In Bay Bridge traffic
a fresh look at the world, its microbes and investigators
who introduced me to hot and sour soup
I needed
the ribcage of epidemiology
protecting vital organs of public health
even as police tear gassed protestors on campus

East Oakland, you gave me the weariness of wet winters
coldness creeping into my bones
chaos creeping into my brain
a reminder of my true home
in the desert where I could liberate the past
under blue skies
bury the war we didn't want
yet even now
we find ourselves
tripping over its bones

AFTER MATH

you went quickly
into your boots and stetson
new records and radio station

I lived longer
in the last decade
and wavered
between tweeds and jeans

but these days I find
I need the heel and hat
the rough denim on the legs
I keep for walking
soft flannel on the chest
next to where it hurts

I understand
finally why
you picked these fabrics
to keep
from ripping apart
at the seams

UPON LEARNING OF THE DEATH OF MY EX HUSBAND

pain of every color
pierces my body
lightning strikes of
ice and fire

I am lost though I've been here before
the map is missing
always a blue moth hovering
around the flame of regret
flits around conversations never mended
smoldering untended

seasons of memory
with large arrays of color
spearing the ground for rumors of gold
gems and buried treasure
I drive these old roads
where the map is missing
where friendships die
where nothing new is ever built
where gravel can still fly into windshields
and snowflakes
climb into winter

at the end of the road
everything that remains
is the color of snow
the color of salt
is the color of bones

FOR JOHANNAH

my daughter is a foreign country
I have arrived
as an immigrant
to her land
of time and language and custom
with jet lag
deaf to the sounds around me
and speechless
reaching for the wrong spoon
asking for an unknown condiment

she beckons to me
¡mira mama!
even after more than a year
she is
still a devoted guide
to my ignorance

pulling me down to whisper her secrets
pushing me on to more discovery

I shall learn the customs here
the rhythm, the staccato, the pause
my ears and mouth will synchronize
in time
I may even learn to dance

MIENTRAS

I am never alone
dead lovers climb into my bed
walk in and out of my house
move books and jewelry around
steal whatever they want
I walk down familiar streets
and ones in cities I never knew
greeting people in languages I never knew
past rice fields and tennis courts
climbing into attics full of trunks
full of photographs of people I don't know
houses that belong to me with rooms
I have forgotten and objects I have missed
casual acquaintances wait for me
to pick them up at an airport in the rain
or a bus station at night
I am driving an old Peugeot
with a yellow steering wheel
and a faulty second gear
there are forests of tall pines
and ones oxygenated with bamboo
beaches full of tourists
and vacant beaches with black rocks
holding tide pools of invertebrates
I am every age and so are the people around me
I know the people I belong to
but they all look different
speak languages I now understand
and when there are no people
I belong to the families of lizards and birds
and when there are no animals
I belong to the families of trees
My closest relatives are
the red dirt and the round stones
and when they are gone
I belong to the wind and the stars

AT A TIME

the past is a foreign country
of strange customs and echoes
we sneak in and out
with expired passports
when the wind is a certain way
when the planets align or moonlight shines on the sheets
the past knows
we no longer belong
but turns a blind eye to occasional intrusions
as long as we cause no trouble
what we see there
is draped in diaphanous fabrics
filaments of soft light
we cannot explain
tin types of people we knew
remnants of music once loved

the future is another name
a secret name
the book of names
is either on a shelf we can't reach
or hidden behind many locked doors
in labyrinths
it's possible the book never existed
or the blank pages are waiting
for silent scribes in white silk robes

we are here now with the crows
who recognize us
know neither our past
nor our future
they remember
whether we are enemies
or friends

IDENTITY

identity is an orphan
seeking a home
that doesn't exist
living in a body
brought to us
by barefoot ancestors
we never knew
and didn't choose

people call us a name
but it is never our real name
we have forgotten our real names
but remember the names of grandchildren
we will never have in this lifetime

people say we are from a country
that we also
didn't choose
maps shifting
names of countries shifting
we are not from here

the streets and roads
of our dreams
have no names
and still
we walk them
speak to the ghosts who meet us there

DRIVING THE MIMBRES ON A WINTER DAY

dark wet limbs of leafless cottonwoods
cast new Henry Moore sculptures, curving
stark against a winter sky

stark against the tawny hills
rising from the river
against the white light
of snow on the Black Range
high above juniper dotted hills.

thick January clouds are
interrupted by patches of blue sky

sporadic snowflakes dance in the wind
die on the windshield

light fractures
emphasizes the difference
between snow and tree bark
between sun and cloud shadows
fragments that move with the wind
move with the miles

luminosity
light so magical
I wish to claim it
not to hold
only to inhale

DRIVING WITH THE SPIRITS/ MANEJANDO CON LOS ESPIRITUS

these highways, these roads,
these paths along animal tracks
have been traveled before me
in conveyances from feet to fleet
and in front, rises the road that meets the sky
I travel secure with one or more beloved spirits
who have crossed the meridian moon,
traveled further than I

we share this time together
I cherish the memory of each
and each mile of the landscape

some of them want to kiss me
some to apologize
or raise old grievances
sometimes they want music
they don't know we are stuck with the radio signal
or my own poor pitch voice
one of them wants Neil Diamond
another Willie Nelson
one more wants Death Cab for Cutie
and I want to hear "Sweet Dreams Are Made of This"

no matter distractions,
they notice things
a deer jumping suddenly from the left
a hawk diving toward the windshield
a blind or icy spot…
it might have been
too late without them
and I too could cross the moon meridian
but this time
I am kept alive
give thanks with my breath

certain that the luminous threads
that connect our past
connect our future

these are my spirits
I travel with them
on worn paths
traveled before us
they know where we are going

ON OUR ROAD

in one week
bear and elk lost lives
in place of woman and man

do the creatures bestow, in dying,
their animal powers
to the drivers of their deaths
or become vengeful chindis?

the terror of murder
and the shame of survival mingle
mixing blood and fur
with mangled metal

horror lingers past
the image of impact
followed by passing cars,
flashing lights, shock, and tears
horror can last for years.

smaller animals,
squirrel and skunk,
collide with cars more often
but they don't have the power
to kill us on the road

ADVICE TO MY SON

You must find your ancestors
wherever they are:
in stones, rivers, trees
in countries, dreams, music
among people you never knew
lines, even boundary lines
the provenance of power and time
of mapmakers and skin
melt into metaphor
themselves mere inventions of the mind
where we belong cannot be dictated
you may make your bed anywhere
anywhere   that is   where it is   possible
art and love make all things possible

we may have thought our existence stops
where our skin stops or
where life begins and ends
every lover proves this wrong
love and disease
memory and trauma
haplogroups and mutations
travel like black swans
like devout pilgrims, like migrants
like refugees
like stones thrown into lakes

we only measure what we can imagine
clarity is hardly an option
even in rocks, especially in people
ambiguity sneaks in and out
of every gene every molecule every pore
ribboned and sealed in packages meant
to convince us the world
is uncluttered

SILENT SONATA: WINTER

today's light falls
as large hypnotic snowflakes
create more light
on a windless winter day
cloud and sky exchange colors
a silent symphony of notes
falls on the brown ground
lands on green pine boughs
and leafless branches

the nopales in the yard
have white blooms

underneath the warmth of darkness and quilts
desert winter sounds are white
barely audible but
they creep into consciousness

the instruments of winter
play soft sad notes
on pillows
where only memories of music
are stored

FRAGMENTS OF A SPRING FANDANGO

Paco Peña in the background on classical guitar
traveling 45 miles an hour
on a highway only 25 miles long

grey green lace of spring
cottonwoods
emerge from the dark brown limbs of winter

pink and white orchard blossoms
begin a show of promise
often compromised
by wind or winter blowing them off course
easily just as we are

I hear a small airplane overhead
look up
there is a large hawk sailing
and the plane is behind me

evening comes and I am
restless in sleep
allow the dark moons
of the universe
to pass through my body
with each breath
tides wash this bed of dreams

SUMMER SYMPHONY

the August sheets are sour with the smell of sweat
imaginary ants keep my dreams disturbed
even the dog has found another room to lie in
there are crickets inside and out
there is dry lightning in the distance
and farther away is any hope
that the rains will come

I put water on the tree with one pear
I put water on the tree with two plums
I put water on the tree with ten peaches
I eat the plums and peaches
the pear disappears
I harvest three miniature carrots
that grew alone in a long row
the pomegranate with a plethora of blossoms
and verdant branches yielded no fruit

finally, the sky growls, then barks
with flashing lights leading the way
and the horses come galloping across the land
throwing up pebbles on tin roofs
trees waving at them
I sit at the window with a terrified dog at my feet
neither of us able to sleep
listening to rain barrels fill and arroyo rushing
watching rivulets run
and, finally the horses tire

a gentle mist grows grasses and weeds
green hair growing everywhere
these rains have sprouted
seeds and weeds and morning glories
growing in places
no one has planted them   ever

optimism and despair
the two songs of summer

AUTUMN DINING CONCERTO

after summer rains,
October sky where the only cloud
is a half moon
the rest a bowl of cerulean soup

cottonwood leaves are jeweled gold coins
falling along the river path
turning café au lait as they lay unspent

tamarisk, apricot feathers that
stroke away the sweat of summer

grama grass, the beginning
of soft cinnamon sugar sprinkles

mountain maple and Virginia creeper turn scarlet
scrub oak, molé colorado

bare limbs and dead branches scratch menus
in every language on cobalt slates of sky
blue plate specials

peach tree leaves become lips
colored by the peaches
that have long been devoured
ombré, kissed by real lips

toasted with champagne love-
shaped hearts from lilac and aspen

the pines stay their salads of greens and bluegreens
elms are tablecloths
of old ivory lace

sky dancing

fall is always perfect
but it never lasts

HARBINGERS

we made such a mess this winter
the vultures have returned
to clean up after us
last year I took a photograph
of vultures roosting in a tree
near Lake Roberts
from a distance their shapes
are formidable, yet friendly
close ups are not so flattering

very distant comely cousins
hummingbirds migrate hundreds of miles
brave unpredictable wind and wetness
to spend warm months in the Mimbres
you may hear them
but see them only if they are close

the humans with their calendars
mark the arrival of both species
get the binoculars out to be sure
clean and fill the feeders

vultures and hummingbirds
their arrival means spring
one eating sugar water and nectar
the other, the dead

THE WIND

in April, the wind
brings gales of memory
throws pebbles of the past
in my face
threatens my gait

birds flap their wings and go nowhere
blossoms fly off fruit trees,
limit this year's harvest
tumbleweeds and years pile up along
barbed wire fences,
refuse to budge

in April, the wind
reminds me
through dust
my life has not been tidy

THE GREAT DIVIDES

I live **on** a divide
that geographic line
that separates oceans
a Continental Divide
that skips across the tops of mountains
from northernmost North America
to the southernmost South America
from the Bering Strait
to the Strait of Magellan
and along this line
rain that falls, snow that melts
on one side travels to the Pacific
on the other to the Atlantic

some days I am on one side
other days on the other
most days, however
I am in a zone that goes nowhere
so little rain, so few places
for water to go except back
to her home in the sky
inland desert places
can be like that
salty

I live **in** a divide
a divide of peoples
culture, language, custom
harder to navigate
than the CDT
and on this trail
I walk on both sides of the line
but live in the salty playa zone
nowhere to go and no desire to leave

I live **with** a divide
the wild and thorny trail I forged so many years ago
is now a smooth path I walk every day
accept all the pieces of myself, somber and silly
cherish my fractured history
succulent and salty

RIBBONS OF RAIN

You could
hold ribbons of rain
between your cloud hands
let wetness slide
through your fingers
onto earth's dry skin
soften the land
with blankets of green
and wildflowers of every color

I could
feel the wind ripple through
native grasses
and dance
barefoot with abandon

once I thought that
love would be
like this

THE TRICKSTER MOON

how can I trust the moon
if it might not be there
                                        unless I look at it?
and how will I know
where to look for the moon?
because it is
in a different place every night
                                        [if it exists at all when I am not looking]

I have never trusted the moon
for exactly that reason
and it changes color and shape
nearly every day
sometimes it shows itself
even in the day sky
but when I look for it there
it isn't

however, there is worth
in even an untrustworthy moon
that magic trickster, shapeshifter
whether it is there
or not there when I am not looking

so maybe, quizás
if I want to keep my moon real
I have to keep looking
maybe I have to keep looking
at everything I want to keep real

CLOUDS

In August I fell in love
with clouds
their defiance of gravity
their shape shifting prowess
faces of ancestors, animals
how they mass and move with wind, with magic
mobiles, *alebrijes* in the sky
I fell for the colors of clouds:
in early morning: pale pinks bright yellows
at sunset: scarlet and apricot, or the opposite
when clouds, purple and swollen, are ready
to deliver a sound and lightning show
a deep fake
        whip the wind into symphonies
        that end in crashing cymbals
or in earnest
        on the dry desert
        dropping inches of rain
        while arroyos run wild and muddy
in August, clouds write their own haiku each hour anew
draw maps of new countries
and ignore old boundaries
roll in waves across mountain shore lines
I love them white and fluffy
with underbellies of tarnished silver
in bold streaks across the sky
clouds that contrails suddenly burst from
and clouds in asemic squiggles or smoke signals
that could be messages waiting to be understood
this is why
I fell in love with clouds
the same way
I have always fallen
in love

COYOTE SCREAMS INTO MY DREAM OR WERE WE METAPHORS

I am asleep
Coyote dying or dying to mate
is telling terrifying bedtime stories
while she swallows
sharp tortilla chips
and flaming hot Cheetos
that Owl drops from a thundering sky
Afterwards, Coyote screams
but keeps eating
and Owl keeps dropping chips
pausing only for her own last supper
Coyote continues eating and screaming

I clutch the blanket around me in fear
and curl my body into a fetal position
Coyote is real, Owl might be real, I am real and afraid
Hours until silence
Coyote is alone, maybe dead
Owl is alone, I am alone, alive

I thought the dream was about Coyote
but was it really about Owl
or all three of us?

DARKSUCH DANCING

We huddle together in dreams, in tall stones braced against the wind
in mountain streams that run and run dry
leave pebbles and dew
clues along long untraveled paths

you are the mute swan in the lagoon angling to the left
I am in a foreign country but not lost
awake still dreaming, still swimming in silver
the barest hint of you
leaves a towel resting on the bank

this train you are traveling
is cold and very dry
it hurts to blink or breathe
where are we going
now that I am here?
you unfold the map in your pocket
squint and try to decipher a strange alphabet
tiny snowflakes attack your window sideways
the wool blanket you are wrapped in is scratchy and coarse
It may have fleas
you share it
even though I am invisible

a scrawny cat emerges from a house
living or dead
I watch a wizened Apache
with deer dance sticks in his hands
gaze into the eyes of the cat
brush my cheek twice with a feather

we huddle together in dreams and are
restless on the nights when sleep is elusive
the skunk is back in the neighborhood
but the scent of you is closer still
the fragments of song
of hawks of words weep
while we dance a limping waltz

BRAIDING THE LONG HAIR OF DARKNESS

braiding the long hair of darkness
sequestered from the fractal light of day
and fiery sunset
she wraps winter blankets around
her body clothed with flannel pajamas
and wool socks
lays the book and glasses aside
extinguishes lights of the house
except for a fire in the wood stove
that has been banked for the night
the lights in the sky blink on
clouds move through
a rounding moon
the fingers of darkness
work through the night
weaving the dreams
that come unremembered
but for now she is caught
in the dark braids of longing
that always seem to be
ephemeral clouds
moving through moonlight
and moving on
leaving her frigid stiff fingers empty
at dawn

SPACE/TIME MASH UP

this time it is dark
I was crawling through concertina wire
around a camp in Quy-Nohn
uncertain which side of the war
I am on
but it doesn't matter
no one will know I am here

another time
I fall into the depths
of a black hole or a cenote
you might think there is no escape
but there is
aways an escape

once there was a meadow
lit with sunshine and flowers
a stream runs through it
and a mountain lion growls in the distance
We will have skipped school that day

there is often a familiar house
it has rooms I have forgotten
I discover them anew
and rearrange the furniture
Valentín will come to prune the trees

two children played
with a slinky on the steps
its coils triggered a glimpse
of all my pasts, all my futures
and a déjà vécu now

MESSAGE IN A BOTTLE

I wave goodbye to the past
with words
that are
accompanied by lyrics and beats
of the oldies

        craft my phrases tenderly
accord memory its last rites

take from a box some paper
        write words
        scratch some out
        ponder them

roll them up
tear-stained and bloody
kiss them goodbye
and stuff them in bottles

set them a sail
        to land on unknown shores
        or drown alongside ship wrecked sailors

this house is full
of bottles waiting
to be filled
and the music is always playing

SOME MEMORIES

some memories are set in concrete nailed to fenceposts
travel through time with us clear as the moment it happened

some memories take us to places we could find without maps
directions unfurl in our minds, we need no luggage

some memories fade over time, fog envelopes them
a scream becomes a whisper and the whisper is muffled by the wind

some disappear in daylight but unreel at night
chasing us as packs of wolf memory, hungry, howling

some memories soften. liquify with time
we savor them as fine wine or a sip of tequila, and smile

some wave patriotic flags, others burn them
some stomp into the day refuse to leave, others shy children
who must be coaxed with sweets or other promises

some memories are feathers that tickle the edge of consciousness
dance with ringed fingers and tiny bells, pull us into forgotten arms

some memories are old friends or old enemies who we welcome now
they keep us company when so few of us are left

some memories no longer exist. can someone tell me
how my mother sounded when she answered the phone?

some memories bring us to cool water or hot beach sand
forests with wild raspberries or mushrooms
canyons of red sandstone, pathways to the ancients

some memories bring dogs chasing balls, dying fish, injured cats, birds
that flew away
disappearing lizards and kangaroo rats, flashes of fur, shiny scales,
falling feathers

we eat some memories: first taste of an artichoke, frog legs
the time we cracked lobsters with pliers
a shrimp cocktail in Guanajuato, escargot in Berkeley

some memories are mere inventions
some reach out a hand and declare: this dance is for you

ADOBE WORDS

your voice falling after this thunder
like handfuls of cool mud
plastered onto silence, our lightning wounds

dark mending over the places
that will always need it:
a result of exposure or poor planning

your words soothe and dry in place
tadpoles make a magic appearance
after the storm

add more water to the cracks
in the sun, on the surface
smooth the mud
with your weathered hands
and pray for a climate
that cures us slowly

Cheryl Howard, Ph.D. lives, writes, and creates multimedia art in the Mimbres Valley of southwestern New Mexico. Her paternal grandparents left Tennessee and homesteaded in southeastern New Mexico. Cheryl has lived most of her life in the southwest and has always considered New Mexico home. This is the place and these are the people who sing to her. However, she has lived in several additional states: Colorado, California, Massachusetts, Virginia, and El Paso, Texas. She studied English and Psychology as an undergraduate at the University of New Mexico (UNM) in Albuquerque, and later worked at the School of Public Health at UC/Berkeley while a Vietnam-returning, now deceased husband finished out his tour of duty. After that, she returned to the Medical School at UNM and worked there in rural health and cancer research for many years before remarrying and starting a graduate program in Sociology at UNM. During her years in Albuquerque, she wrote, published, and performed poetry, in addition to publishing scientific articles. Artistic endeavors were curtailed during her time of raising a family and teaching at the University of Texas/El Paso. After retiring, she has resumed writing and artistic activities with a passion. She lives on a little more than an acre of land with her border collie and a dozen chickens; she has an Airbnb and a big messy studio.

www.ingramcontent.com/pod-product-compliance
Lightning Source LLC
LaVergne TN
LVHW090539110826
845146LV00003B/1183